# HEALING

ASHBURNHAM INSIGHTS

# *Healing*

A re-reading of Scripture by

**TIMOTHY PAIN**

**KINGSWAY PUBLICATIONS**
EASTBOURNE

ISBN 0 86065 533 4

Unless otherwise indicated biblical quotations are from
the Jerusalem Bible, copyright © Darton, Longman & Todd Ltd
and Doubleday & Co. Inc. 1966, 1967, 1968

*Cover photo shows front water
and the main bridge at Ashburnham Place
(colour photograph by Judges Postcards Ltd, Hastings).*

Printed in Great Britain for
KINGSWAY PUBLICATIONS LTD
Lottbridge Drove, Eastbourne, E. Sussex BN23 6NT by
Cox & Wyman Ltd, Reading.
Typeset by Nuprint Ltd, Harpenden, Herts AL5 4SE

# *Contents*

# Foreword to the Series

I am very pleased to commend this series of *Ashburnham Insights* which have come from the pen of Timothy Pain. Those of us who have watched developments at Ashburnham Place over the last few years have been particularly intrigued with the way things have developed. The careful thinking in these volumes comes from a background of faithful believing prayer for many years, and a deep concern for renewal and revival.

When there is an emphasis on experience, and when the subjective element in Christian living is to the fore, there is more need than ever for scriptural foundations. That is why we should be grateful to Tim for the obvious care he has taken to 'test everything', while at the same time to obey the apostolic injunction to 'despise not prophesyings'. Both should play their part in balanced Christian living.

Tim is not afraid to break new ground. I like the living way he writes, and I am sure these small books will have the wide readership they deserve.

*Canon Michael Harper*

This second set of four short books is dedicated to the memory of my grandmother, Mrs A. T. R. Jones (1894–1986).

This obstinate old East-Ender knew nothing but hardship and suffering throughout her long life. After twenty-two months of marriage she was widowed at twenty-two; Nan never recovered from this, yet lived on sixty-nine years to see thirteen of her fourteen great grandchildren. The twin sacrifices of her war-widows' pension and her wonderful praying supported many in Christian service.

# Introduction

The developing series of *Ashburnham Insights* has been inspired by members of the Ashburnham Stable Family. This is a Christian community which is part resident at Ashburnham Place (a Christian training centre) and part scattered throughout the villages and small towns of East Sussex. It is our calling to maintain an unbroken 'Chain of Prayer' within the Palladian Stable which is adjacent to Ashburnham Place. We pray, by day and night, for the renewal and spiritual unity of all Christian churches in East Sussex. It is our firm conviction that the only hope of the world is in the renewal of the church, and as one expression of this we have taken it upon ourselves to share in a serious re-reading of Holy Scripture.

About ten thousand people visit us annually, and our observation and participation in hundreds of conferences has led to our conclusion that much contemporary teaching is based more on experience than on the Bible. Just as we have gained courage from each other to move from the shifting sands of tradition and experience, so we urge you to excavate and stand firm on the solid rock of Scripture.

The first set of books dealt with four issues which relate to the inner life of a local church—prophecy, tongues and explanations, intercession and baptism in Holy Spirit.

And in each slim volume I mentioned that these subjects have some evangelistic aspects. This second series deals with some facets of the life of a local church outside of the rows and semi-circles of saints on Sunday—blessing and cursing, healing, deliverance and counselling. And these four books are unashamedly evangelistic in their emphasis.

I fear that today we have two false preoccupations: one, the eternal massage of the souls of the saints; and two, power. I am sure that these books would sell much better if they were entitled 'Power healing for believers', 'Power deliverance for believers', 'Power blessing for believers', and so on. But they are written by a weak, fallible, ignorant and very vulnerable human being who is part of a community characterized by weakness, infirmity, foolishness and wordly insignificance, which is itself surrounded by thousands of people going to hell. Fortunately the members of the Ashburnham Stable Family have discovered that God's power is at its best when wrapped in human weakness. We are quite content with our frailty and infirmity but are sufficiently discontented with our unbelieving friends' eternal destiny to get up off our plastic chairs and follow the Poor Man of Galilee out into his weeping world.

This book is humbly offered as my personal re-reading of Scripture about healing. It has been lived in, worked out and written down in community, and it is the product of much study and prayer, reading and listening, experimentation and embarrassment, banter and disagreement. A few within the Stable Family still lovingly disagree with one or two of my conclusions. Some of the material was originally worked on with the Rev Edmund Heddle for our leaders' training days, and other parts were worked on with Mr Ralph May for our ten week training courses. The final format is my own responsibility.

I have written the *Ashburnham Insights* with house-group leaders uppermost in my mind, and all the material has been refined through constant usage in groups of multiples of four. I have tried to write in a way that is simple enough to satisfy my wife, but is sufficiently thorough to persuade the local clergy. The Scripture references must all be looked up and examined as you proceed through the text.

Any acclamation should be shared between John and Marlis Bickersteth, Helen Brown, Sheila Day, Edmund Heddle, Gay Hyde, Roger Kemble, Sue Lindsay, Jo and Susie Marriott, Margery May, Ralph May, Alan Pain, David and Edna Parr, Catherine Rendall, Barbara Stidwill, Roger and Penny Wilcock and my wife Alison. Their prayers, patience, comments, research, advice, encouragement, work and love have brought these four Insights to publication.

*Timothy Pain*

The renewal lives by the re-reading of the New Testament.

*Cardinal Suenens*

Back to the Bible or back to the jungle.

*Luis Palau*

O Lord and Master Jesus Christ, Word of the everlasting Father, who hast borne our griefs and carried the burden of our infirmities: renew by thy Holy Spirit in thy church, we beseech thee, thy gifts of healing, and send forth thy disciples again to preach the gospel of thy kingdom, and to cure the sick and relieve thy suffering children, to the praise and glory of thy holy name. Amen.

*A traditional Greek eucharistic liturgy*
*of the Church of Alexandria.*

Honour the doctor with the honour that is his due in return for his services; for he too has been created by the Lord. Healing itself comes from the Most High, like a gift from a king.... The Lord has brought medicines into existence from the earth, and the sensible man will not despise them.

*Ecclesiasticus 38:1–4*

The world is sick, and yet not unto death;
There is for it a day of health in store;
From lips of love there comes the healing breath—
The breath of Him who all its sickness bore,
And bids it rise to strength and beauty evermore.

*Horatius Bonar*

# Healing

Twenty years ago, in 1966, the spiritual plaudit 'alive' was regularly awarded to those local churches which held frequent gospel services and weekly prayer meetings and saw occasional converts. Today that same plaudit is normally reserved for those local fellowships which hold regular ministry times and weekly house groups and experience the occasional healing.

Twenty years ago, prayer for the sick meant requesting God to guide the local GP and hospital staff as they cared for those too ill to attend the services. Today, prayer for the sick appears to mean asking God to heal (or commanding healing—it depends which conference has been attended) those people who are well enough to attend the meeting, but would like to feel even fitter.

Twenty years ago our pulpits were pounded by post-Graham pastors pleading with absent sinners 'to get up out of their seats'. Today our over-populated platforms ring to another cry as post-Wimber preachers call for 'more power Lord; more power', hoping that some unsuspecting saint will slump down *into* his seat.

God, by his gracious Spirit, has put healing at the top of many ecclesiastical agendas. Large numbers of books on healing have been written and read. Few committees dare organize a conference without a seminar or two on healing. Everybody knows somebody who once saw a dramatic healing. In some churches I am now too frightened to cough, lest a great wave of hands descends upon my furrowed brow.

Healing services and ministry times continue to proliferate, and some people are healed. Amidst the wildly exaggerated claims there is a hard core of healthy people who have discovered the truth that the living God still heals today. For every sick person untouched by medicine and healed by God I shout a loud hallelujah, but the reality of their existence should not blind us to two glaring facts. Firstly, that the overwhelming majority of people ministered to, or prayed for, are not healed; and, secondly, that a charismatic tradition, technique and vocabulary of healing has emerged which is more rooted in experience than in Scripture. This book addresses these two problems. I believe that the God of the Bible can and does heal today. I have been privileged to observe several authentic, lasting and remarkable healings; but I am convinced that the church needs to re-examine the Old and the New Testaments to establish a few principles of healing which could save us from wandering down some blind alley in misguided over-enthusiasm.

This book is deliberately narrow in its scope. It deals only with what has come to be known as 'physical healing'. There are three companion volumes which deal with the associated areas of deliverance, counselling and blessing and cursing. I do not pretend that physical healing is the totality of the church's ministry of healing, for the church is called to take the healing of the cross to every sector of our sick society, not just to those with broken bodies. But as the Holy Spirit seems to have drawn the church's attention to physical healing in a new way, it seemed good to focus exclusively on this one aspect of healing.

Through the centuries there have always been those individuals and movements which have cured the sick, and we should be particularly grateful to the Roman Catholic Church for keeping alive both a belief in and an experience of Christ's healing power. However, it is true that in this century there has been a widespread rediscovery of this element of the good news. In the early years of the twentieth century two strands evolved: an Anglican interest developed in a sacramental approach to healing which stressed the laying on of hands and anointing with holy oil; and the growing Pentecostal movement emphasized the 1 Corinthians 12 gifts of the Spirit.

From the first direction God used groups like the Guild of Health, the Divine Healing Mission, the Guild of St Raphael, the Lambeth Conference of 1930, the Churches' Council for Health and Healing, the 1953 Archbishops' Commission on the Churches' Ministry of Healing and the considerable influence of books by Leslie Weatherhead and Francis MacNutt. And from the other direction he used notable personalities like William Branham, Smith Wigglesworth, Charles Price, Kathryn Kuhlman, and more recently Jean Darnall, Harry Greenwood and Ian Andrews.

Today there is a growing convergence and mutual appreciation of these two influences, touchingly exemplified in the ministry to the dying David Watson by both Bishop Morris Maddocks and John Wimber. The two styles of ministry are not alternatives, for each has strengths that the other lacks. Each tradition needs to learn from the other, but both need to expose their ideas and practices to the scorching light of Scripture.

This book is not a recipe for instant success, nor is it an attempt to build one single vehicle for healing out of the Rolls Royce of sacramentalism and the Maserati of pentecostalism. Instead it is meant to be a healing Highway

Code—relevant regardless of the vehicle in which God
has placed us.

# Healing in the Old Testament

The Old Testament reveals Yahweh, the God of Israel, as a God who heals. Promises of healing (Exodus 15:26; Deuteronomy 32:39; Psalm 103:3; Ecclesiastes 3:3; Isaiah 19:22; 30:26; 57:18–19; Jeremiah 30:17; Hosea 6:1; Malachi 4:2); prayers for healing (Psalm 6:2; 41:4; Jeremiah 17:14); testimonies of healing (Psalm 30:2; 107:20; 147:3); perplexity about a lack of healing (Jeremiah 15:18)—all of these abound. In particular, nine incidents are recorded from which we can begin to develop an understanding of how God occasionally intervenes to bring about a miraculous healing.

## Abimelech

The biblical introduction to healing is found in Genesis 20 where God healed King Abimelech, Abimelech's wife and all the women of his household from impotence and barrenness. Abraham was the human agent involved in the healing, and in this chapter God identifies him as a prophet.

It is the first mention of a prophet in the Bible and establishes the clear scriptural association between prophets, intercession and the miraculous, including healing, which it is so vital for the church today to appreciate.

Genesis 20 also suggests the idea that some sickness can be sent by God as a curse or punishment, but that through intercession God may revoke his action. We cannot know the time-scale involved in this miracle but several weeks must have passed before the harem had convincing proof that they had been cured. I am not arguing that this sets a precedent for gradual healing, but it does indicate that a delayed appreciation of healing is not without scriptural foundation.

## Miriam

The second incident, recorded in Numbers 12, tells the story of Miriam's healing from leprosy, and repeats each of these three ideas. The prophet Moses was God's agent of healing; Miriam's sickness was a punishment sent by God; and it was a week before the healing was revealed to anybody. This incident introduces another element which is only hinted at in the Abraham story. Miriam was given responsibility to perform an action to facilitate her healing: she had to remain outside the camp for seven days. In Genesis 20 Abimelech had to choose between returning Sarah and death, and he then went beyond that to give cattle, sheep, slaves and silver. Perhaps this compensation helped bring about the healing?

## Jeroboam

The third story introduces the place of fasting in healing and teaches the lesson that the healing agent must obey God's orders absolutely. In 1 Kings 13 an anonymous Judaean prophet, who was under a divine order to fast, denounced the altar at Bethel that King Jeroboam had

made for a golden calf. An angry Jeroboam ordered the
seizure of the prophet, but God instantly withered the
king's hand. Jeroboam knew the principle that only a
prophet could both placate God and bring healing, and in
verse 6 he urged this prophet to do so. The nameless
prophet interceded with the Lord and the king's hand was
instantly healed. But within a few hours the healing
prophet lay dead, mauled by a lion. Why? Because within
those intervening hours he had been deceived into dis-
obeying Yahweh's injunction to eat or drink nothing.

## The Zarephathian

1 Kings 17:7–24 tells the story of Elijah's stay at
Zarephath. His landlady's son died and she attributed her
misfortune to Elijah. She believed that the presence of a
prophet had illuminated her secret or unconscious sins
and drawn down divine retribution. Elijah took the body
and carried it to his own bed. Then he cried out to God in
prayer, and how he must have prayed! For Elijah, unlike
all his successors, had no precedents: there had not yet
been a resuscitation. 'He stretched himself on the child
three times and cried out to Yahweh, "Yahweh my God,
may the soul of this child, I beg you, come into him
again!"' God answered the prophet's prayer and Elijah
gave the revived boy back to his mother. The first of the
eight biblical resuscitations had just taken place.

## The Shunammitess

Elisha, who inherited a double portion of Elijah's
prophetic anointing, is the supreme healing agent of the
Old Testament. 2 Kings 4:8–37 relates the two episodes
involving the Shunammitess' son. This anonymous woman
of rank in Shunem had been hospitable to Elisha and

Gehazi, and this prompted Elisha to offer to put in a good word to the king of Israel on her behalf, but she proudly replied that the benevolence on her own people was adequate. So, instead of a material reward, Elisha announced, in the name of the King of kings, that she would give birth to a boy in twelve months' time.

Again this was a prophet at work: not, this time, begging God to act, but acting as God's executive authority, prophetically announcing what would happen. Once more there was delay, for she could not have been certain of conception for five months. But here there was no note of censure as this woman did not need to be released from the curse of barrenness; it was her elderly husband who needed some divine assistance!

## The Shunammitess' son

The boy was born, developed normally, then suddenly dropped dead. But the Shunammitess' faith in Elisha remained absolute. He had obtained a son for her, therefore he could restore him; so Elisha was visited. He gave Gehazi his staff and sent him to stretch it over the corpse, but nothing happened. So Elisha came himself, went into the bedroom alone with the body, and prayed.

On this occasion the healing agent had to perform an unusual task to aid the healing process. Without anyone watching or knowing, Elisha climbed on to the body and lay on top of it; when the cold flesh felt warmer he stepped off. Elisha walked to and fro, then clambered on the corpse again. Seven times he repeated this performance, and then the dead boy sneezed. The second biblical resuscitation had occurred.

## Naaman

The healing of Naaman, 2 Kings 5, was another cure initiated by a request. The Aramaean army commander, together with his team and chariot, drew up at Elisha's house. This time the prophet merely sent a messenger with the details of the God-given task Naaman had to fulfil. Naaman's indignation, in verse 11, has a curiously contemporary ring to it: 'Here was I thinking he would be sure to come out to me, and stand there, and call on the name of Yahweh his God, and wave his hand over the spot and cure the leprous part.' It is almost as if Naaman had attended a mid-eighties 'signs and wonders' training conference! Yet Naaman had to learn that healing is not a matter of technique, but of obedience; and that sometimes God calls the one requesting healing to comply with a command. Naaman's pride was pricked by his servant's words and he obediently immersed himself seven times in the river Jordan. This was a gradual, but complete, healing of a mild skin disease which did not preclude social contacts.

A grateful Naaman recognized that Yahweh alone was truly God and pressed Elisha to accept a present. He refused. The agent should take no reward or credit for something that God alone has done. So instead of thanking man, Naaman praised God and collected enough Samaritan soil to build an altar to Yahweh in Damascus. He rode off in his chariot, healed and blessed, the first convert through a healing miracle.

## Elisha's bones

The fourth healing story to involve Elisha is a most uncomfortable miracle for many Protestants. 2 Kings 13:20–21 is another resuscitation, yet goes unmentioned

# St Francis Xavier—sixteenth-century apostle of the Indies

Francis Xavier was one of the greatest missionaries who has ever lived. He was born in 1506 at Navarre, and at the age of twenty-nine became a disciple of St Ignatius after an enormous personal struggle. In the following year he nearly died on a winter journey through Germany. Surgeons declared him incurable, but his three companions prayed through the night and he was restored to health. Following this he gave himself to working and praying for the incurably ill in a hospital for the dying.

At the age of thirty-six he sailed as a missionary to the Indies and in 1542 was part of the extraordinary revival at Goa. It was there that he realized God still miraculously healed people. Francis travelled on to Sri Lanka and made little evangelistic impact until a woman who had been in labour three days gave birth following prayer. Many were converted through this incident and he began regularly seeking God for signs and wonders to endorse his preaching. Travelling down the Pearl Coast he saw an astonishing series of healing miracles—including four resuscitations which are recorded in great detail.

He moved on to Travancor, where he received the gift of tongues and saw thousands converted, but none healed, until one day near Cape Comovin when he was in a village which was hardened to the good news. Prompted by the Spirit he prayed that God would honour the blood and name of his beloved Son, and ordered some bystanders to open the grave of a man who had been buried the day before. Already the body was putrifying. Francis fell on his knees, prayed, and commanded the dead man in the name of the living God to arise. The man arose in perfect health.

He travelled on to Japan still seeing hundreds saved wherever he went, but very few miracles. He died at the early age of forty-six trying to reach China. His dead body was taken back to Goa and records state that: 'After touching his body several blind persons recovered their sight, and others, sick of palsies and other diseases, their health, and the use of their limbs.'

at most healing conferences. Out of fear of the raiding Moabites, some Israelites tossed a dead friend into Elisha's tomb. The body bounced against the bones of the dead prophet and sprang to life! Yahweh is not a tame God: we cannot imprison him in the straitjacket of a healing technique. Time and again God works miracles through individuals and in ways which we find both inappropriate and embarrassing.

We should not pretend that these verses are not in the Bible but neither ought we to build upon them a healing technique of venerating the bones of deceased prophets and urging sick people to touch them. We dare not dismiss the thousands of well-documented cases throughout church history when God appears to have used a similar means in authentic divine healing. Such verses and incidents should teach us humility and openness.

## Hezekiah

The last Old Testament healing miracle, 2 Kings 20:1–11, was of King Hezekiah's near fatal ulcer. The prophet Isaiah came to announce imminent death. Hezekiah wept and pleaded with God—and God changed his mind. So Isaiah was sent back to announce three things: a healing which would take place in three days' time; a fifteen-year life expectancy; and the immediate prospect of peace for Jerusalem. Here the healing agent was given an unusual task. Isaiah summoned a servant, ordered a fig poultice, applied it to the deadly ulcer, and the king recovered, but disbelieved. He asked for proof, and Isaiah supplied it.

These nine incidents reveal much about the sovereignty and power of God, but little of a healing pattern. However, certain principles emerge which we can take with us into the New Testament. In the Old Testament, healing was the exclusive activity of God's servants the prophets.

Occasionally, but only in a minority of cases, the sickness was due to sin. Normally, but not always, either the agent or the client needed to do something which would advance the healing. Ordinarily the prophetic agent either begged God for the healing, or announced its imminent arrival. Usually an element of faith, or expectancy, was present. However, sometimes none of these applied and God intervened in his inimitable, sovereign way.

# *Jesus the Healer*

At the time of Christ there was a Jewish expectation that the coming Messiah would be another prophet like Moses, who would fulfil Moses' prophecy in Deuteronomy 18:15–20. Jesus was universally recognized by friend and foe as 'a prophet' because of what he said and did. (There is a fuller demonstration of this in the *Ashburnham Insight* book, *Prophecy*.) In Acts 3:22–24 Peter showed that he believed Christ to be 'the prophet'. Jesus Christ was the supreme prophet, mighty in word and deed; and because of this he was also the supreme healer of all time.

Many have been reared with the understanding that Jesus healed the sick and performed wonders because of his deity. But the response of those who observed his miracles was not to name him as God, but to identify him as a prophet. In John 9:17 the Pharisees asked the entertaining beggar what he had to say about Jesus now that he had opened his eyes, and they were given the swift reply, 'He is a prophet.' John 6:14 makes it clear that the hungry thousands fed by five loaves and two fish leapt to the same conclusion.

Jesus was the perfect Son of God from the moment of his conception, but we have no hint that any of his contemporaries suspected a divine origin or prophetic office.

But all this changed after the anointing with Holy Spirit at his baptism. The Holy Spirit came upon him to commission him and equip him for his messianic task. There is a striking parallel here. In 2 Kings 2 Elisha begged for a double share of Elijah's spirit. He received this when he placed upon his shoulders Elijah's cloak, which had fallen from the sky as a sign of the Spirit. We have no record of Elijah healing anyone other than the boy at Zarephath, but Elisha became the great healer of the Old Testament. John the Baptist was recognized by Jesus as the second Elijah, and he healed nobody. John baptized Jesus in water and Jesus received a mighty anointing of the Spirit to become, amongst other things, a second Elisha—a great healer.

Jesus left the Jordan, left John, was driven into the desert by the Spirit, faced satanic temptation and then returned to his home synagogue to announce himself as the fulfilment of Isaiah 61:1–2. The local carpenter proclaimed that he was now going to give new sight to the blind. And he did.

The 39 books of the Old Testament list nine healing miracles. Jesus, the supreme prophet, has overtaken all the Old Testament prophets by the twelfth chapter of the first gospel. The gospel writers accredit twenty specific incidents to Jesus the healer. These are (1) John 4:43–54 (2) Matthew 9:18–26; Mark 5:21–43; Luke 8:40–56 (3) Matthew 9:20–22; Mark 5:25–34; Luke 8:43–48 (4) Matthew 9:27–31 (5) Matthew 9:1–8; Mark 2:1–12; Luke 5:17–26 (6) Matthew 8:1–4; Mark 1:40–45; Luke 5:12–14 (7) Matthew 8:5–13; Luke 7:1–10 (8) Matthew 8:14–15; Mark 1:29–31; Luke 4:38–39 (9) Luke 7:11–17 (10) John 5:1–18 (11) John 9:1–41 (12) Matthew 12:9–14; Mark 3:1–6; Luke 6:6–11 (13) Luke 13:10–17 (14) Luke 14:1–6 (15) Luke 17: 11–19 (16) Mark 7:31–37 (17) Mark 8:22–26 (18) John 11:1–44 (19) Matthew 20:29–34; Mark 10:

46–52; Luke 18:35–43 and (20) Luke 22:47–51.

Then they record twelve general statements about the activity of this great healer. These are found in (1) Matthew 4:23–25; Luke 6:17–19 (2) Matthew 8:16–17; Mark 1:32–34; Luke 4:40 (3) Matthew 11:4–5; Luke 7:21–22 (4) Matthew 9:35 (5) Matthew 12:15–16; Mark 3:10–12 (6) Matthew 14:14; Luke 9:11; John 6:2 (7) Matthew 14:34–36; Mark 6:55–56 (8) Matthew 15:30–31 (9) Matthew 19:2 (10) Matthew 21:14 (11) Luke 5:15–16 and (12) Luke 8:2.

From these two sets of passages we can begin to ask and answer some questions which should mould the Old Testament ideas about God's healing into durable principles which are relevant for the church today.

## Who was healed?

The twenty detailed incidents mention thirty-one people healed by Jesus: twenty-four men, three women, three children (two boys and a girl) and one servant whose sex is unknown. The emphasis is on men being healed. My observation is that contemporary healers have reversed this emphasis. In most services and meetings that I have attended it is mainly women who are prayed for: this is borne out by the examples in books on healing. Now I am not suggesting that we aim to heal fewer women, simply that we become less reserved about ministering to men.

The Old Testament prophets healed those in authority, the privileged few—kings, an army commander, a woman of rank, a high priest's sister. But Jesus specialized in healing beggars and social outcasts: nineteen of the thirty-one healed by Jesus—over 60%—were the scum of society. No prestigious adult is presented as an example of healing, merely two children and one servant of those in authority: the remainder were common people suffering from terrible afflictions. We need to recapture this stress and turn our healing attention to the tramps, addicts, gypsies, AIDS victims and other pariahs of our society, without neglecting the great mass of ordinary working people who fill our tower blocks and estates.

## What were they healed of?

Biblical healings were dramatic, incontrovertible, and obvious to even the most cynical. Jesus healed quadriplegia, paraplegia, a severed ear resulting from a sword wound, a withered hand, twelve blind eyes, eleven lepers, two severe fevers, one distressing gynaecological disorder, chronic curvature of the spine, dropsy, someone who was deaf and stuttered, one who was agonizingly paralysed and at the point of death, two who had already died and one whose corpse was decomposing. The general statements add that he healed the epileptics, set the lame walking, the dumb talking, and made cripples whole again. 'He went round...curing all kinds of diseases and sicknesses among the people...and those who were suffering from diseases and painful complaints of one kind or another...were all brought to him, and he cured them' (Matthew 4:23–26).

So many of today's meetings seem to specialize in migraines and leg lengthenings (which no matter how closely I peer I always fail to notice) whereas Jesus does not appear to have healed ailments which were merely inconvenient, nor those matters which the primitive medicine of his day could deal with. He cured chronic suffering that caused isolation and loneliness; disorders which prevented social contact and employment; ailments which had persisted for great lengths of time; and people near to either side of the point of death. We would do well to remember these things. I know that our Father can number the hairs of our head, but I do not think this means that he is concerned primarily with healing things as trivial as baldness, coughs, colds, toothache, headache, spots and those things which are easily dealt with by contemporary medicine. (Though it is nice when he does!)

## Where were they healed?

Jesus did not hire the temple for a healing service, advertise in Jerusalem guaranteeing signs and wonders, book the apostolic band to lead the worship, preach a sixty-minute sermon, call out 'words of knowledge' or appeal for the sick to come up to the communion rail. He healed people wherever they were. Most were healed whilst Jesus was on a journey. Four were healed in the privacy of their own beds. One was healed in a garden, another at a dinner party, one at his own funeral, another in his grave, one at a house meeting, another at the Jerusalem equivalent of Lourdes. Only two of those we are told about were healed at an organized, pre-arranged, religious meeting—in the local synagogue.

I am sure that one reason for the lack of lasting, tangible success in our healing meetings and services is that we are trying to heal in the wrong place. God seems to delight in healing at the roadside, in healing in the course of daily living, in healing social outcasts who will never attend religious meetings. We should remember this principle if we want to share in the 'greater things' promised by Jesus.

The general statements which describe Jesus healing large crowds of people who gathered round a house are no justification for advertised healing crusades or services. Jesus did not seek crowds; the crowds sought him. They came to inconvenient locations at unsocial times. We experience little of this. Our pre-arranged, expensively-advertised meetings (with a love gift for 'vital expenses') are full of Christians seeking the latest in spiritual entertainment. They bear no resemblance to the occasions when diseased and crippled Galileans shuffled to the house where the poor carpenter was staying.

## How were the healings initiated?

I believe that the answer to this question establishes a principle which, when followed, proves enormously helpful in the church's healing ministry today. Jesus' healing miracles were, without exception, always initiated in one of two different ways. In this Christ followed the footsteps of his prophetic forebears, and set an example which was continued by the church right through to the early years of this century.

Christ only healed in response to either a man saying, 'Please heal me,' or God, by his Holy Spirit, whispering, 'Go heal him.' In twelve of the twenty specific incidents the initiative was an unsolicited 'Please', seven times by a friend or friends and five times by the individuals themselves. I suggest that the initiative in the other eight incidents was the Father prompting the Son to go to a particular individual at that unique moment to take healing to him.

Jesus did not heal everybody, but he did heal all who came to him asking for healing, and he did heal particular individuals selected by his Father. We have no record of Jesus asking people to express a desire or need for ministry of any kind, and we would do well to follow this pattern. The contemporary practice appears to be for attempted healing to be normally instigated in one of two different ways. Either the priest or preacher invites those who want healing to indicate this in some fashion, usually by walking to the front or altar; or people call out 'words of knowledge'. These are usually illnesses or injuries, and those suffering from such a condition are urged to identify themselves. Neither of these two practices has any foundation in the Scriptures and both support the erroneous view that Christian meetings and a human response are prerequisites for divine healing.

Healing needs to be initiated by God: either by the Spirit urging a person to request healing, or by the Spirit instructing the human agent to offer healing to a particular individual, but not by some half-cock hybrid midway between the two. I do not believe that what are commonly called 'words of knowledge' are normally anything more than embryonic promptings of the Spirit. It is ludicrous to think of Jesus at the pool of Bethzatha calling to the crowd, 'Is there anybody here with paralysed legs?' All Old and New Testament healers identified the individual not the ailment; they expected the Spirit to guide them directly to whoever the Father sovereignly wanted to heal at that moment in time.

We do not have any definition of the 1 Corinthians 12 spiritual gifts, merely the indication from their context that their primary use is in the public worship of the church. It seems to me from the context that the attributes of the Spirit listed in Isaiah 11:2 are much more appropriate designations of the Spirit's work in ministry and counselling. (Please see the *Ashburnham Insight* on counselling for a fuller discussion of this point.) Jesus demonstrated all of these attributes in his healing ministry, but it is often pointless to attempt to identify which particular attribute he revealed in any given incident. He merely went, did and spoke whatever the Father prompted. I think it would greatly help the church's healing ministry if we suspended the slipshod use of the term 'word of knowledge' because the present use educates believers into a false and restrictive understanding of a precious gift, and actively prevents the church from moving towards a more Christ-like healing ministry.

I am not suggesting that those who speak 'words of knowledge' as an initiative for healing are necessarily wrong. I know of an increasing number of instances when the 'words' have been most precise and the speaker knew the name and appearance of the person about whom they spoke. However, they should have exercised their Spirit-given initiative, and used the knowledge to go directly to the person, instead of waiting endlessly for an unnecessary human response.

I am suggesting that the phrase 'word of knowledge' is the wrong label for this type of speech. And I am urging that those who speak imprecise words should never be content with their awareness of an ailment, but should ask that God would guide them directly to the person to be healed, realizing that what they have is only tentative and embryonic.

### How were they healed?

The Old Testament prophets either interceded for healing or announced the imminent arrival of the healing. Jesus, whose life was soaked in prayer, did not publicly inter-cede for the healing of an individual. He knew that he could do nothing by himself, but could only do what he saw the Father doing (John 5:19). So Jesus restricted himself to whatever he understood the Father to be doing. His acts of healing were usually either by touch, command, announcement or a mixture of the three. In eleven of the twenty recorded stories Christ touched the person. This was not what is meant by 'the laying on of hands' (a phrase which conjures up bizarre images in my mind!). In the Bible, hands were placed on the head of an individual for blessing, for the anointing with Holy Spirit, and for commissioning for special service; but not for healing. It is better to think and speak in terms of 'the healing touch' rather than 'the laying on of hands', and to do as Christ did which was to touch gently the affected part of the body.

It is fashionable at the moment not to touch the person, but to hold or wave the hand some six inches to a foot away from the person. This curious custom has no basis in Scripture where we are clearly instructed to place our hands upon the sick, not to let our hands vibrate near the sick.

In four of the eleven instances of touch it was sufficient for Christ to touch the person. Twice he touched and added a command (these were two of the resuscitations). Three times he used saliva in conjunction with the touch. In one of these incidents the person healed was given responsibility for a task to assist the healing—he had to bathe in the Pool of Siloam. Once Christ rebuked the illness before touching the person, and after an exorcism he both announced the arrival of the healing and touched the person. (There is more about 'rebuking' and 'exorcism' in the *Ashburnham Insight, Deliverance*). Christ twice healed a person who was some miles away from his physical presence, and on both these occasions he announced or gave a promise of healing. Five times Christ spoke a command of healing: each time in a case of immobility due to death or paralysis. And three times he instructed the people to do something which would help bring about the healing.

The story of the haemorrhaging lady who touched the tassles of Christ's cloak is an enigma. It is one of several New Testament equivalents to the 2 Kings 13 resuscitation. I could understand it if she had touched his hand, but a tassle! God delights in mysteries. This pricks the bubble of my intellectual pride and increases my charity towards those whose methods I disdain.

Many today have predictable patterns of ministry, but that was not Jesus' way. In every situation he only did what the Father instructed, and that meant something different with each person he healed. We ought to learn from him and discard our techniques and systems; saturate ourselves in preparatory prayer for guidance, boldness and empowering, and then do what the Father says—and no more—and only for those to whom he directly sends us, or those whom he sends directly to us.

## What happened after the healings?

After healing a person Christ often demonstrated his compassion by giving helpful and practical advice. This is shown by his instructions to Jairus and his astonished wife to feed their twelve-year-old daughter, and by the way he returned to reveal his deity to the John 9 beggar after hearing of the man's excommunication.

Four times Christ ordered silence about the miracle. This is important advice that we would do well to repeat today. Many try to help God's work by pressing for premature public testimonies, both spoken and written. This is not God's way. He heals because he loves and cares for the individual, and not normally as a means to another end. God delights in the secrecy of the incarnation, whereas we prefer noisy fanfares. My experience suggests that there is a correlation between premature testimony and lapsed healings; I believe this area needs further research and examination.

Only once did Jesus press for publication of a healing, but that was to remind the ten lepers to visit the medical authorities for ratification of their healing so they could return to normal society.

In this push-button age we foolishly look for short cuts in evangelism. Healing primarily demonstrates God's

## Graham—from a small rural village
## near Hastings, East Sussex

In March 1986 Graham was told by his doctor that he had a cancerous growth in his nose which, along with the bone, would have to be removed within two weeks. He returned home to his wife, crying and very frightened. That night he went to the local pub to drown his sorrows. As soon as he had gone Linda, his wife, telephoned a Christian who lived nearby. She urged this local believer to come and pray with her. The believer came, talked with Linda, and realized that in her distress she was ready to trust in Christ. Gently she led Linda to God.

Then Graham returned home and was most surprised to see one of the local 'religious' people sitting in his living room. The believer asked if she could pray for Graham. He was too embarrassed to refuse and the praying lady commanded the growth to go in the name of the Lord. She committed Graham and his fears to the Lord and left.

As soon as the door closed Graham exploded: 'Why did you invite her? I don't believe in all that rubbish. The only one who can heal me is the doctor!' Linda was convinced that God had healed Graham. The local believer was convinced that she had made a total fool of herself, that she had done everything wrong, had been terribly insensitive, and had probably put Graham off God for life!

Two weeks later the doctor examined Graham at the local hospital; looked shocked; checked and double-checked; then pronounced himself baffled. There was no sign of the cancerous growth. It had vanished.

Linda, in the excitement of her new-found faith, said, 'I told you so!' Graham wanted to believe that God had healed him, but could not accept it. Ten months on from the healing Graham appears to be as far away from God as he has ever been; however, his nose is still perfectly whole.

sympathy with the sick, and only secondarily does it substantiate the spoken message. A sensational healing does not necessarily convert anybody. Spectators or relatives were converted in only one of the twenty gospel incidents: in John 4 the nobleman and all his household believed when the son was restored to health. Twice we read that the news spread, once that the people admired Jesus, and on two occasions they felt awe. But in so many instances the reaction was antagonistic: twice there was persecution, once there was opposition and argument, and another time there were plots of destruction. The chief priests determined to kill Christ after the raising of Lazarus, and seized him as Malchus grew a new right ear. Perhaps most remarkable—yet the same thing happens today—is that five times there was no reaction at all to one of Christ's wonderful gracious healings.

Not even all the people who were healed turned to follow and believe in Christ. Certainly Peter's mother-in-law served Jesus, the John 9 beggar worshipped Jesus, the nobleman's son believed in him, and Bartimaeus was saved. But only one of the ten lepers returned to Christ. The other nine went away healed, but still not saved.

And it was not always so wonderful for those who had been healed: some were plagued with questions; the John 9 beggar was excommunicated and his parents almost were. Poor Lazarus had the most difficult time of all. Firstly, people rushed to view this walking phenomenon, then the chief priests decided to assassinate him because of the numbers who flocked to see him!

Right through his three brief years of ministry Jesus was busy healing the sick. But he was doing something else as well: he was training the twelve disciples and the other followers in his healing ministry. We will now examine how well they learnt from Jesus of Nazareth, the supreme healer.

# The Healing Early Church

The staff was the symbol of Old Testament prophetic authority. When Elisha sent Gehazi to raise the dead boy, he equipped him with his staff as the sign that Gehazi was acting in the name and authority of a prophet. Gehazi had previously observed a healing miracle and only had to do exactly as his master had said. He did, and yet nothing happened. How I sympathize with him!

Jesus followed Elisha's pattern with his own disciples. First he ensured that they had been with him whilst he healed. Then he invested them with his authority to cure the sick themselves, but this did not take the form of a staff—rather they were to bear the power of Christ's own name.

Luke 8:22–9:6 shows how the mission of the twelve immediately followed the calming of the storm, the exorcism of the Gerasene demoniac, the cure of the haemorrhaging lady, and the raising of Jairus' daughter. Matthew 10:1–16, Mark 3:13–19 and Luke 9:1–6 give the detailed instructions for their mission, with Matthew identifying the six pairs who worked together. They were told where to go, what to do, and how *not* to finance the trip. They went healing, ejecting demons, blessing every household and proclaiming the good news everywhere.

At the conclusion of the tour they returned to Jesus to give him an account of all they had done; and he withdrew with them to Bethsaida so that they could have time to themselves for prayer, refreshment and appraisal.

These events were closely followed by Peter's profession of faith at Caesarea Philippi, Christ's announcement that upon this he would build his church, and the transfiguration. Then Christ expanded his healing ministry to include seventy-two other disciples. Again they were sent in pairs to definite locations, with instructions to bless, heal, preach the good news, with the life expectancy of stray lambs which had wandered among a pack of wolves. We have no details of any specific incidents from their pre-Calvary exploits, but Jesus' exasperated comment, 'How much longer must I be among you and put up with you?' in Luke 9:40–41 indicates that these early healers were not always completely successful.

In the three years of ministry before his death Jesus modelled and multiplied his healing work so that at least eighty-four people were involved. These individuals healed in pairs, using the delegated authority of the prophet Jesus. It is important to note and recognize that, as far as we know, between Palm Sunday and Pentecost these eighty-four healed nobody. In Acts 1:4–5 and Luke 24:49 we read that Jesus pressed them to stay in Jerusalem until...until they, in their own right, received the prophet's equipping of the anointing with Holy Spirit. Before Calvary the early followers of Christ healed as types of Gehazi; after Pentecost they healed in the succession of Elisha—as fully-fledged members of God's prophetic, healing community. Before Pentecost the Holy Spirit was only sent upon a select few; since Pentecost he has been freely available to all who are in Christ. (There is a fuller discussion of these points in the *Ashburnham Insights* on prophecy and baptism in Holy Spirit.) Those, and only those, who have been immersed in Holy Spirit possess the necessary power and authority to bring God's healing in the same successful manner as the Old Testament prophets and Jesus.

## Who, what and where?

Acts records eight incidents of healing: 3:1–10, 9:8–19, 9:32–35, 9:36–43, 14:8–10, 19–20, 20:7–12, 28:7–10; and six general statements: 2:43, 5:12–16, 6:8, 8:4–8, 14:3 and 19:11–12. From these I conclude that the early church followed the principles laid down by the Old Testament prophets and Christ.

The people healed were a collection of beggars, social nonentities, opponents, friends and one aged relative of the wealthy Prefect of Malta. They were healed of long-standing, untreatable, very debilitating diseases: for example, dysentery, death, acute concussion, paralysis, blindness, etc. These cures took place in a wide variety of locations—once on the way to a prayer meeting, three times in a private house (two of these were in the course of normal sick visiting); once during an informal open air rally, and once out in the countryside after an attempted assassination. The only healing to take place at a pre-arranged, regular meeting of the church was the resuscitation of Eutychus at the regular breaking of bread in Troas on the first day of the week, but then he hadn't been ill prior to that meeting—and urgent action was called for.

## The initiation

It appears to me that the early church followed Christ's principles of initiating a healing miracle. The general statements suggest that they ministered to all those who

41

came to them requesting healing. Seven of the eight specific incidents show that the first Christians were ready to minister at the Holy Spirit's prompting. Appeals by the apostles, inviting people to come forward for healing, are conspicuous by their absence!

The middle-aged man of Acts 3, who had been lame since birth, always begged at the Beautiful Gate. Peter and John must have passed him dozens, if not hundreds of times; so too must Jesus. Yet the man was still immobile. I assume that he had never asked Jesus or any of his followers to cure him; all he wanted was money, he had no higher expectation. We cannot know exactly how Peter was prompted to say what he said, but in some way the Holy Spirit informed him that the man was to be healed and that he was to speak the words. Peter and John had not left home intending to heal anybody, they were going to a prayer meeting. But when the sick man was carried past somehow they knew that they had to bring God's healing to him. Maybe in the past they had mused that it would be good if God healed that man; perhaps they had prayed that God would heal him. Nobody knows. But they heard and obeyed God's voice.

Ananias is an enigmatic figure, yet we owe him so much. He was a simple Damascus disciple who anticipated imminent arrest. We do not know if he had ever healed anybody before Acts 9:10, but I think it improbable; God threw him in the deep end of ministry! Ananias' vision was startling in its clarity and detail. He did not like what he saw, and he told God so. God rarely informs us what will result from obedient action: normally he demands compliance regardless of the consequences. But Ananias was a beginner, Saul was a special case, and so God gave to Ananias an insight into what could happen through his unconditional obedience. So Ananias shut his front door and walked to Straight Street to restore the sight of one who held a warrant for his arrest.

Aeneas, who had been bedridden with paralysis for eight years, was visited by Peter. It does not appear to be anything other than part and parcel of Peter's regular visitation. I guess from the context that there had been no previous healings in Lydda. Peter stood over Aeneas and was informed by the Spirit that God was about to cure this paralytic. Peter had been anointed with Holy Spirit at Pentecost, and this intimation was merely God keeping the promise found in Amos 3:7–8. Peter announced, as a prophet, what he had just been told. And it was so.

Within a few days two visitors arrived from Joppa, some twelve miles away on the coast. They brought news to Peter that a favourite saint had died and that many were greatly distressed. They begged for a pastoral visit as soon as possible. There is nothing in the verses to indicate a request for a resuscitation. However, Peter was prompted to return with them straightaway and on arrival was taken to Tabitha's body. It is only natural that, on the journey, Peter would have turned over in his mind the possibility of her being raised from the dead. The idea must have grown without becoming a certainty, because the first thing that Peter did was to kneel and pray in privacy. Was it a petition for guidance and boldness, or an intercession for a miracle? I suspect the former. But whatever the content of the prayer, the net result of the praying was that when Peter rose from his knees he knew exactly what he had to do.

A life-long cripple sat in a crowd listening to Paul preach the good news. Somehow the Spirit so worked in the man's life that he believed he could either be saved or cured. It is unclear what he expected, but he desired something and sought Paul's attention. Paul saw the unspoken 'please' on the man's face and broke off in mid-sermon to shout a healing command. I am not sure whether the initiative here was a man saying 'please', or God speaking 'go'—or both; but it certainly was not a general appeal for the sick to come to the front for prayer. As a result of the miracle, Paul received first an acclamation and then an attempted assassination. The crowd hurled boulders at him and dragged his unconscious body out of Lystra towards a cemetery. Yet within a few minutes Paul was on his feet striding back to town and the next day he walked thirty miles to Derbe. What happened is obscure. The Christians crowded round the body. But did they pray? Announce healing? Touch the body? Or did God work a sovereign miracle without any human intermediary? We cannot know: mystery always pervades God's acts of compassionate healing.

The Sunday meeting at Troas began on the Saturday evening. They met to break bread and then Paul preached a long, long sermon. Eutychus was seated on the window-sill; he grew drowsy, then fell asleep and toppled out of the open window to fall three floors to his death on the ground outside. A doctor was present (Luke himself) and Eutychus was certified dead. But Paul had other information. He was prompted, presumably by God, to take action and announce life. The eighth resuscitation of the Bible was about to take place—the Zarephath boy, the Shunammitess' son, the fearful Israelites' friend, Jairus' daughter, the son of the Nain widow, Lazarus, Tabitha and lastly Eutychus.

The final Acts healing incident took place on Malta. Paul went visiting the sick and called on the Prefect's father who was in bed with feverish attacks and dysentery. Perhaps, like Peter with Tabitha, Paul had an inkling of what would transpire. So maybe he prayed to distinguish between divine instruction and Pauline enthusiasm; but after prayer Paul knew what God was going to do and what he must do. He obeyed God's 'go', healed the man, and then was faced with a large number of sick islanders saying 'please'. Paul brought God's healing to them too.

## The healing action

In healing, Jesus touched those who were not dead or paralysed. He appears to have reserved words of command or announcement for the severely ill. The Acts incidents indicate that the early church made more frequent use of spoken words, and less use of touch. In Acts 3 Peter commanded, 'In the name of Jesus Christ the Nazarene, walk.' When nothing happened he hauled the man to his feet and let go. What a moment that must have been!

Ananias announced, 'I have been sent by the Lord Jesus so that you may recover your sight.' Immediately Paul could see.

Peter announced, 'Aeneas, Jesus Christ cures you: get up and fold your sleeping mat.' Aeneas got up immediately.

Peter commanded, 'Tabitha, stand up.' She opened her eyes, looked at Peter and sat up.

Paul said in a loud voice, 'Get to your feet—stand up,' and the cripple jumped up and began to walk.

Paul clasped Eutychus to himself and prophetically announced, 'There is no need to worry. There is still life in him.'

Only with Publius' father's dysentery (and perhaps also Paul's recovery from acute concussion) was touch without words used in healing.

The general statements in Acts 5:12 and 19:11 suggest the use of touch in association with healing, but these verses present many problems. They are the early church equivalent of Elisha's bones and Jesus' tassel. Aprons and handkerchiefs which had touched Paul were taken to the sick, and the Jerusalem and district incurables tried to position themselves so that some portion of Peter's shadow passed over them as he walked by. Luke, the author of Acts, suggests that this odd behaviour was honoured by God and empirically successful. What I have written about the bones and tassel also applies to these incidents. There is mystery here. Such events underline God's sovereignty and should increase our openness to the healing antics of others; but surely it is pointless to attempt to emulate them today, as some try to do.

## The consequences

The Acts healing miracles had a role in evangelism and early church growth. After healing the forty-year-old lame man Peter and John were arrested, imprisoned overnight and severely reprimanded by the rulers, but many of those who had heard Peter's explanation of the miracle became believers. The consequence of Saul's healing was his Damascus preaching which led on into his fruitful future. When Aeneas was healed 'everybody who lived in Lydda and Sharon saw him, and they were all converted to the Lord'. The whole of Joppa heard about Tabitha's resuscitation, 'and many believed in the Lord'. However, the other incidents record little impact for the good news. The healing of the cripple in Lystra led to misunderstanding and persecution. Paul's healing from concussion made little impression. The people were 'greatly encouraged' by Eutychus' resuscitation, but nobody was saved. Many requested healing after Publius' father was cured, but no one turned to follow Jesus—yet another occasion when people were healed in body, but remained dead in spirit.

We have much to learn from the healing early church, but a straightforward implementation of their pattern and technique is inadequate. We need to receive, as they

## Penny Ward—Sutton Coldfield Baptist Church, West Midlands

Teenager Penny had shown great promise as an athlete when she was struck down with the knee condition, condra-malasia patella. She was in continual pain and for the two years up until December 1985 she had walked only with the aid of one—and sometimes a second—stick.

She became a Christian in July 1985 and joined her local church, but was not part of the life in an unbroken way. In November 1985 the leaders of the church discovered the long-term nature of the injury and felt prompted to offer prayer for her healing until she was healed.

At the first communion service in November a small group prayed for Penny. A leader touched her knee and others touched her head. As they prayed she crumpled to the ground and sobbed. It appeared that the hurt and frustration of the injury was being released. During the following week the minister visited Penny's parents to share the church's hopes, expectation and commitment. They were received with warmth and friendship.

Two weeks later another small group prayed for her at the communion service; again she fell to the floor, but this time there was a real aura of peace.

Two weeks later, on the first of December, she was prayed for a third time. Again her damaged knee was gently touched; again she fell to the ground. She lay on the floor for fifteen minutes whilst the small group carried on praying. Then she leapt to her feet and threw away her sticks. She felt stiff, but free from pain.

Within a week she was running and jumping. Two weeks after her healing she was baptized. She is now able to run many miles at a stretch.

Her parents began attending church from the moment of the healing—despite previously having been resistant to the church. On Easter Sunday 1986 they committed their lives to Christ and have since been baptized, as has Penny's twin sister.

received, the prophet's anointing of healing power from on high without which we are as impotent as Gehazi. But many today who have received that anointing still have not seen God endorse their words with authentic, biblical, healing miracles. I believe that we need to examine the two contexts within which Jesus and the early church healed, so that the church's healing ministry today can be set against a similar background.

# The Context of Biblical Healing

When Jesus revealed in the Nazareth synagogue that he was the fulfilment of Isaiah 61:1–2, he was not introducing himself only as a healer of the blind and the broken-hearted. The passage made it clear that his primary calling was to bring the good news to the poor. The anointing of the Spirit upon the Old Testament prophets was essentially to equip them to speak God's words. Jesus' anointing at his baptism was given for the same purpose: he became God's mouthpiece.

## Evangelism

When Jesus began to speak in that synagogue he won the initial approval of all, for they were astonished by the gracious words that came from his lips. 'This is Joseph's son, surely?' was their perplexed question. They were mystified by the change in speech that they noticed in the person they only knew as a local carpenter. Right through his years of ministry it was his teaching which made the greatest impression, because of the authority with which he spoke. Primarily the healing miracles demonstrated the compassion and power of God, but they also served to validate what Jesus said and taught. They illustrated what he announced—that the kingdom of God was at hand. Healing cannot be extracted from this evangelistic context without a distortion of both the message and the miracle.

The twelve were sent out to proclaim the kingdom of God and to heal. The two charges were parallel and inseparable. And so the six pairs went from village to village proclaiming the good news and healing everywhere. After that Christ sent out the seventy-two with an identical mission: they were to cure the sick and announce the proximity of the kingdom of God. And that is exactly what they did.

The early church kept the two callings in tandem. They preached and then healed; or they healed, quickly followed by a spoken explanation. This was one secret of their phenomenal growth. On a slightly wider basis than healing, church growth in Acts is fourteen times attributed to the association between signs, wonders and the proclamation of the gospel; six times growth of the church is precipitated by signs and wonders alone; and only once (at Corinth) is this growth directly related to preaching alone. Surely this should be enough to suggest that a right and natural context of healing is alongside the proclamation of the good news to those who, as yet, do not belong to Christ. Certainly Paul thought so in Romans 15:18–19.

Very few of those healed in the New Testament were followers of Christ. Paul, Lazarus and Tabitha were disciples, and perhaps so too were Aeneas, Eutychus and Peter's wife's mother, but the other thirty-two do not appear to have been followers at their healing. Some were interested, others were curious, many believed that Jesus could cure them; but they had not yet forsaken all to follow him. This is not the situation today.

In this country we are faced with meeting-centred, rather than people-centred, evangelism; and we have indiscriminate attempts at healing the saints, rather than the healing of selected sinners. I am not suggesting that we should never heal in meetings, or never heal believers. But I am pressing for the primary place of our healing to be in shopping precincts, not on sacred pews; in public houses, not in charismatic jamborees; in the High Street and not the holy sanctuary. I am asking for healing to take place firstly at work or in Woolworths, in gardens or garages, in launderettes or lounges, and only secondly on Sunday in services. I am arguing that we make Acts 4:29–30 our prayer and plead with God to enable us to speak his word with great boldness, and that accordingly he will stretch out his hand to heal and perform signs and wonders through the name of Jesus.

A few argue for meeting-centred healing by suggesting that now Jesus is not physically present, his body in its local expression (gathered in rows or semi-circles) carries on his work. The problem with this argument is four-fold. Firstly, empirically it does not work, the success rate is miniscule. Secondly, very few unbelievers ever attend such meetings so it is the saints with headaches who get prayed for. Thirdly, surely the local expression of Christ's body is as real and potent when it is spread through the district in mission as when it is gathered for worship. And fourthly, such healing services give a wrong emphasis on a clerical or priestly ministry of healing. By their nature the focus is on a few specialists rather than on the prophetic people of God.

I believe that one of the two fundamental reasons why so many people who are prayed for are not healed is that we have divorced healing from evangelism. This biblical context has been ignored by charismatics of every shade and opinion, except the Pentecostals. Though John Wimber emphasized this point, many have made his training seminars a model for their healing services instead of taking his principles out into their parish.

## Simple lifestyle

There is a second scriptural context of healing which is as important as the first. Jesus did not commission the twelve only to preach and work wonders, but to do these things out of a lifestyle of astonishing simplicity. They were to take nothing for the journey: no staff, haversack, bread or money; not even a change of clothes. The Poor Man of Galilee had first exchanged the glory of heaven for a lowly Nazareth hovel, then secondly had turned his back on its relative luxuries as he embraced the simplicity of the hedgerow. His anointing with Holy Spirit coincided with his repudiation of material comfort. He healed with no hope of earthly reward, and did not claim expenses or expect a love offering. He taught people to live like the flowers and the birds—with no worries about provisions and total reliance on the Father to define and meet all material needs. Jesus perfectly demonstrated a life lived in dependence upon God for everything. He trusted his Father for food, clothes, direction, words and healing power; and he calls us to follow in his footsteps.

When Jesus sent out the seventy-two he selected them from among those who had followed him on the understanding that a fox had greater security than the followers of the Son of Man; and from among those who had left the dead to bury the dead so that they could go and spread the news of the kingdom of God. Christ called them to a life of total simplicity: no purse, no haversack, no shoes, no choice of food or drink, and whilst living like this they were to cure the sick and effectively prepare the way for him.

Luke 22:35–38 makes it clear that Christ's followers never lacked anything on their evangelistic tours, but it also poses the question of whether this context ceased to apply after the Last Supper discourse. I believe that Jesus was here preparing his followers for the hostile future they were to face. (A similar fate is hinted at in John 17:14–16.) I think Jesus used grim irony to show the intense danger the disciples would face when they went out, not on another rehearsal, but in deadly earnest. The disciples misunderstood Jesus, took him literally and produced two swords: so Jesus rebuked them for their stupidity with an 'enough of that'. Perhaps Christ did mean that the purse and the haversack were to be a means of support when people were hostile and did not provide hospitality. But whether these verses are to be understood as irony or taken literally, the disciples had to expect trouble. They needed their cloaks to keep them warm on the chilly nights, and any instruction to exchange them for swords would have meant great physical hardship.

Whichever way Luke 22:35–38 is taken, we still need to live simply if we are to proclaim the good news successfully through preaching and healing. The testimony of Acts makes this clear. In Acts 2 the Jerusalem converts owned everything in common, sold their goods and possessions and shared out the proceeds among themselves according to what each one needed; and the same practice was followed in Acts 4:32–35. Peter and John must have set the example, because in Acts 3 they had no money. I do not think Peter had just forgotten his collection money, I believe that he still had either no purse or an empty purse. Is it too much to assert that this miracle would not have taken place but for the apostles' simplicity of lifestyle?

Many western Christians wonder why God seems so eager to bless their third world counterparts with an abundance of miraculous healings, and yet is so reluctant to heal in the West. I think that it is not a question of belief, faith, technique or tradition, but is due rather to the difference in lifestyles. The many waves of monasticism provide a clear example of this principle. Each wave began as a movement of God's Spirit committed to prayer, evangelism and a very simple life. In the early years of each new order God confirmed their words with large numbers of miraculous healings. But as the years went by the movements were corrupted by wealth and assumed a life of comparative ease; and so the miracles ceased. At times there almost appears to have been a direct correlation between the degree of self-sacrifice and the number of healing miracles! In the past some Protestants viewed the Catholic records of these healings with suspicion, but that was in a day when healing was virtually unknown in the Protestant experience. I have placed old records of monastic miracles next to authenticated recent accounts from the third world and found the similarities striking. In charismatic ears they have a ring of truth.

Third world Christians today tend to have a view of the world that does not preclude the supernatural dimension of Christianity. Some have isolated this fact and suggested it to be the real reason for their greater experience and blessing in the realm of the miraculous. I disagree. Clearly it is one factor, but not, I think, the primary one. I believe the essential reason for the difference between western and third world Christianity in this area is that they have set the healing ministry of the church in its two correct biblical contexts of evangelism and simple lifestyle. We have not. Some say that when we adopt their world view we will gain their experience. I think that is blind optimism. Instead I assert that only when we identify with the poor in the way we live, repudiate materialism and share the simple lifestyle of the Great Physician will we be promoted from the ranks of those who pray for the sick to join the company of those who heal the sick.

# The Church's Healing
# Ministry Today

The healing ministry is open to every Christian believer. In Matthew 28:18–20 Jesus commissioned the eleven disciples with these words: 'All authority in heaven and earth has been given to me. Go, therefore, make disciples of all nations; baptise them in the name of the Father and of the Son and of the Holy Spirit, and teach them to observe all the commands I gave to you.' Right to the end of time all disciples in every nation are to be instructed to obey all the orders which Christ gave to the original twelve. And this surely must include their evangelistic commission to heal the sick.

In the Old Testament only those select few who had been anointed with Holy Spirit—the prophets—were eligible for the healing ministry. Since Christ baptized the church in Holy Spirit at Pentecost the healing ministry has been a possibility for all believers, whether male or female, black or white, Jew or Gentile, ordained or lay, old or young. The only stipulation is that the Christian believer has been anointed with Holy Spirit. Some will heal more than others; a few will receive a particular gift of healing; most will heal infrequently; but every member of God's prophetic people can be an agent of healing. We should avoid styles of ministry which give the impression that only the ordained, the leaders, or a special few up front can bring Christ's healing.

## Preparation for the healing ministry

### Prayer

We all know the need for much prayer, yet still pray so little, and I believe that this lack of preparatory prayer is another reason for the failure of some contemporary ministry. My rough guide is that, perhaps, an equal amount of time should be spent in prayer as is anticipated will be spent in ministry. This prayer should feature intercession for boldness along the lines of Acts 4:29–30, and silent listening, waiting for God's prompting about ministry.

I find meditation and asking God specific questions to be the most helpful features in my preparatory praying. Uncertainty is a greater problem than disobedience for most people, and the necessary ability to recognize God's voice is enhanced by these two practices. Prayer should be offered essentially for direction and guidance as to the who, how, when, where and what. The prayer should take place beforehand; its primary use is not during ministry.

Many find it helpful to add fasting to prayer. Those who are serious about a simple lifestyle and the evangelistic healing ministry will not neglect this discipline. Fasting need not only be abstinence from food and drink, but can be from anything that occupies our time, for example, sleep, sex, the media, speech and so on.

### Partnership

The principle of partnership pervades the Bible. Christ sent his followers to heal in pairs. One individual alone cannot reflect the image of the triune God; it needs a relationship. The promises of Matthew 18:19–20 are made to two or three, and not to one. Protection from the enemy forces is granted to the church, not to isolated individuals. It should be the norm to minister healing in pairs and quite exceptional to minister it singly. The disciples learnt from being with Jesus when he healed and it is good preparation for us to join with another more experienced. This is the way to multiply the numbers of believers involved in healing.

There are many advantages when we heal in pairs—a geometrical advance in power, more channels for God to use in communication, protection for each other from mistakes. Faith is maintained more easily, courage exists that one person never has, and the flow of ministry can pass from one to another as common sense directs. A member of a pair is precluded from claiming God's work as his own personal achievement and the inevitable failures are shared.

It is best to avoid having more than three ministering to one person as it confuses both those healing and the one being healed. Those nearby who are eager to be involved should sit quietly and unobtrusively, whilst engaging in urgent prayer for the empowering and guidance of those ministering.

*Patience*

Those who bring Christ's healing need an ample supply of patience, for our resources of this virtue are quickly drained by difficult, unlovable people, by delays and by circumstantial problems. The Bible uses different Greek and Hebrew words for these two aspects of patience—towards people and towards circumstances—and teaches different things about them.

We do not need to pray for patience towards people as we already have Christ's patience within us. Galatians

3:27 shows that in baptism we are clothed with Christ's garments, and Colossians 3:12 indicates that one article is his patience towards people. This patience develops naturally from conversion onwards as one aspect of the Spirit's fruit in our life. We need this patience when healing is initiated at unsocial hours; if people are shy, nervous, embarrassed, or take thirty minutes to state the obvious; and when others are rude or rejecting. This patience is part of their cure.

However, we must pray for patience towards circumstances, as this patience is not a free gift at conversion. We should not intercede for our own patience to grow, but for it to be replaced by the patience with which Jesus endured the cross. God slowly develops this in us through our testing, training and suffering and by dispensing it to those who have already stretched their personal resources of patience to the limit.

This patience is necessary to prevent circumstances dictating our response, to enable us to persevere when discouragement comes, to press on to complete results, and to resist the temptation to false intensity and possessiveness of the client.

The healing ministry does not only consist of the recitation of God's words, but it is also the radiation of his love, and we need to be thoroughly prepared with both aspects of Christ's patience if we are to do this.

## Humility

Many are attracted to the healing ministry for wrong reasons. Compassion and obedience motivated Christ. If we hope to ogle at some miracles or be titillated by bodily reactions, we will have been side-tracked. If we plan to send out press reports on what has happened among *us* at *our* meetings, then we will have been diverted. We should seek the holy anonymity of the incarnation and aim to

## Janet Sturt—Hastings, East Sussex

On Christmas Eve 1983 Janet staggered into the midnight communion service at Battle Baptist Church. She had not been inside a church for years and did not know why she had done so on this particular occasion. Her life was a mess: she was in her early forties, was a long-term heroin addict, and because of this had been divorced and was unable to see her children. The people made her welcome and she was referred to Ashburnham Place for help (their minister then lived here). Janet committed her life into God's hands and resolved to stop taking heroin.

Early in the morning of Monday March 5th 1984 I was praying for Janet before meeting her when it was as if Christ particularly drew my attention to Isaiah 41:6–7 and Isaiah 42:18. I was puzzled as I could see no connection between these verses and Janet. Later that morning I and a colleague were talking with her and, as is our habit, we asked her what she wanted God to do in her life. She mentioned that she had been blind in her right eye since birth. Suddenly I felt very cold! Outwardly confident, but inwardly petrified I read these verses aloud. It seemed to me that God was suggesting he would heal Janet's blind eye as a symbol of a deeper work in her life, that there would be many times in the future when neither she nor we would believe that she was free in Christ, but the eye was to be a perpetual reminder of God's work of liberation in her life.

I gently touched her eye and quietly spoke words like, 'Receive your sight, in Jesus' name.' Immediately she picked up a book to see if it had worked. She could see perfectly. Outwardly calm, but inwardly staggered, I continued with the session. I could hardly believe it, and can still hardly believe it. For a few days she had serious problems with double vision as her brain adjusted to two visual inputs!

There have been, and still are, very many times when it appears that God has forgotten about Janet. She has serious difficulties, but the right eye still functions and God's word remains true. She does belong to Christ. Even if a lot of the time it does not look like it!

rivet attention upon God, without basking in any associated glory.

No man can heal another; the highest we can aim for is to be an unprofitable servant whom God occasionally tips off a few minutes in advance of a miracle. We are delivery men, not the manufacturers. Humility is much easier once this principle has been grasped.

The Spirit's work is to glorify, or illuminate the Son. When an ancient building is floodlit it is the building which is admired; the floodlight and rays are necessary, but unnoticed. In a healing miracle the Holy Spirit is the floodlight; our words and actions are the rays of light emanating from, and energized by, the Spirit. Jesus is illuminated and glorified. He it is who must be noticed, not us. He is to be admired, not the mighty deeds. Pride has been the downfall of so many in this ministry. Humility is vital.

## Ministering healing

### Initiation

We have noticed how the initiative for ministry in the Scriptures was always by either man saying, 'Please heal me' or God commanding, 'Go heal him.' There is no good reason why this should be varied today. Since abiding by this principle I have ministered to far fewer people, but seen many more healed. The split in the New Testament healing miracles is exact: half are in response to a 'go' and half to a 'please'. Each one of us should aim to move to this place of balance.

### Interview

In ministry we need to listen both to God and to the client, and this is facilitated by creating a climate of quiet and privacy. Time and again Jesus silenced noise or moved into a private place before commencing ministry. We do well when we emulate his pattern.

Jesus did not function only at a supernatural level, but also at the natural level of observation and deduction. He asked five normal and obvious questions (Mark 5:9, 8: 22–26; 9:14–29; Luke 18:40–43; John 5:6) and if he needed to ask them, so will we.

'What is your name?' The exchange of names is more than mere politeness. It helps to ensure that the ministry is personal and loving.

'What do you want me to do?' This is better phrased as, 'What do you want God to do?' It is an important question as it helps the client to be specific in his request.

'Do you want to be well?' We need to check that he is serious, that he is aware of the consequences of his healing.

'How long has this been happening?' Occasionally the circumstances and background of the ailment need to be investigated to ascertain the cause of the sickness.

'Can you see?' We should establish whether or not anything has happened during our ministry. It is irresponsible nonsense to lay hands on one person and then pass quickly on to the next.

We do not need to know all the medical details, for we are not operating as doctors (this also applies to those who professionally *are* doctors). We only need to know in what way the client suffers and where it hurts. We should not focus on the size of the problem but concentrate on the greatness of God.

As well as questioning the client, it is always necessary to ask God whether anything else needs to be known. He may give us a picture or word to pass on, suggest a statement to make, or put a question into our mind. Sometimes he draws our attention to a non-physical cause, but most sickness and injuries are plainly physical. If God tells us nothing, this means the client has told us everything that we need to know. The interview is complete when the condition has been established and God has told us what to do.

## The cause of the condition

The conditions of Abimelech, Miriam, Malchus, the man at the pool of Bethzatha and the man let down through the roof appear to have had their origin in sin; sin committed either by or against the individual. Many today would demand that Malchus forgave Peter before admitting any possibility of healing his severed right ear, but Jesus was silent about this and healed him unconditionally. Jesus did not insist on a lengthy confession from the unpleasant man at Bethzatha. Instead Christ returned *after* the healing to urge the man, 'Now you are well again, be sure not to sin any more, or something worse may happen to you' (John 5:14). At times, as James 5:16 makes plain, there is an association between the client's confession of sin and his cure, but this is exceptional.

Some teach that a demon always lies behind every ailment, and so demand exorcism before healing can begin. This is true in the sense that death and sickness result from the serpent's activity in Eden, but the Scriptures clearly distinguish between exorcism of evil powers and physical healing, and this difference needs constant emphasis. Ejecting demons and healing the sick are two distinct activities. Sometimes a person may be healed as a direct consequence of the expulsion of an evil power, for example the men in Matthew 9:32–34 and 12:22, but we should not make a general principle from these two isolated instances. In Luke 13:10 Jesus first ejected an evil power, then followed that by touching the woman to heal her bent back; but normally he cured people without any reference to demonic presence or activity.

## Healing actions

There is a natural tendency in all of us to drift into habitual patterns of ministry. However, Jesus was unpredictable. He only did what the Father told him and so his instructions varied with every individual. We have noted the large number of different healing actions used by Jesus and the early church, and we would do well to follow their example of obedient variety and creativity.

Three points are particularly important. First, the laying of hands on the head of an individual is the biblical action appropriate to the ministry of blessing and not to the ministry of healing. (There is much about this in the *Ashburnham Insight, Blessing and Cursing.*) Secondly, prayer for healing should have taken place before ministry. Words of announcement or command, not words of petition or request, should be spoken during the ministry actions. If the initiation was by a human 'Please heal me', then commands like 'Be healed' are appropriate; and if the initiation was by a divine 'Go heal him', a phrase similar to 'Receive your healing' is relevant. Thirdly, God may prompt us to suggest a task for the client to perform, and normally the healing will be delayed until this has been completed, for example, Naaman, Miriam and the John 9 beggar.

## Practical suggestions

I make the following suggestions for those inexperienced in the healing ministry. This model should be constantly varied as the Spirit guides you along his own creative path.

1. Show Christ's love at all times. Smile, use Christian names and relax, for God will perform the miracle, not you.

2. Together with your partner, quietly confess and ask forgiveness of your sins. Only rarely does God work through dirty channels.

3. Ask the Holy Spirit to give you guidance, boldness and power.

4. Keep your eyes open at all times. You are not praying. Christ and the apostles did not minister through interlocked eyelids, and we only receive much necessary information by our observation of the client's reactions.

5. Listen to God and speak whatever he puts into your mind. He may tell you to command a parasitic growth to be removed, or a defective organ to be restored. He may ask you to give a pronouncement of faith or blessing. Keep on asking God questions and listening to his replies.

6. Ask God whether you should touch the client or not. If you are prompted to use the 'healing touch', gently place your hands on the clothing or skin nearest to the affected part of the body.

7. Ask the client, 'Do you feel anything?' 'What is happening?' Ensure that he keeps you informed of the healing progress, or lack of it!

8. Watch for bodily reactions—shaking, stiffening, variation in breathing, falling or sagging, warmth, tingling, hot spots, laughter, weeping, moist eyes, and so on. Though these reactions frequently indicate that God is at work, they are only the body's reaction to God's work; they are not in themselves a work of God. A severe reaction does not evidence a greater work, nor does the absence of any bodily reaction mean healing is not occurring. These things are no yardstick of progress or success. Fifty sunbathers all have different bodily reactions to the same amount of sun. It is the same when the Spirit moves in power. A few always fall over, some shake, but most—as in the gospel accounts—evidence nothing. If a bodily reaction takes place, help the client to

be comfortable, but ignore the reaction and press on with the ministry. The reaction normally ceases before the healing occurs, so do not stop ministering when the client stops twitching or sits up.

9. Continually encourage and relax the client. Tell him of the presence, power and promises of God. Remind him that God made us to be self-healing: if we cut a finger it starts to heal automatically. Suggest a scriptural healing story for him to read out loud.

10. Maintain a flow of ministry between yourself, your partner, God and the client. Whilst one speaks aloud, the other(s) listen to God and the speaker, pray silently for guidance, and watch the client. The lead should pass from one to another as the Spirit prompts and as common sense directs.

11. Silently use the gift of tongues. But if you are stuck and this is obvious to the client, use the gift audibly and slowly. Explain beforehand to the client what you are about to do with words like, 'God has given me a language to use in prayer on those occasions when I do not know how to pray. Neither of us will know what I am praying, but be assured that it is the very best prayer that I could possibly pray for you in this situation as it will be God the Holy Spirit, himself, providing the words I say.'

12. Stop ministering when the client is healed, or when the Holy Spirit tells you to, or when you can't think of anything else to say or do, or when the client asks you to stop, or when anyone appears tired. If the client is not fully healed, arrange to minister again in the near future, allowing time to elapse for further preparation, prayer and fasting.

All this appears to presuppose that the healing will be a long drawn out affair rather than an instantaneous miracle as recorded in the New Testament. Some people—and I am one of them—have a real problem with this. Why the delay? Why the apparent half-healings? Why the regressions? If we suggest that these are only due to our sin or lack of faith it can seem as though we believe that we are personally involved in the mechanics of the healing. But God works the miracle. He brings the cure. We can only announce it.

So why do we need to go on announcing it?

There are many inadequate answers to these questions: sometimes it is more important to God to heal our pride than to heal the client's sickness; at other times his priority is to produce faith in us by developing our patience; and we must remember that this ministry is still being rediscovered after centuries of neglect.

However, I believe that the central reason for delay is that we have foolishly allowed ourselves to be ensnared by the evil one into associating 'healing' with 'power'. We think God wants us to be powerful. We want to be powerful. We covet a 'power' ministry for ourself and our church. And so God has to remind us that he wants us to be content with our weakness, ignorance and vulnerability, and that his strength and power can be seen only when wrapped around human frailty and childlike simplicity. If we ache for God's name to be honoured by instant healings we need to remember 2 Corinthians 12:9–10.

## Advice after healing

We noted earlier that Jesus usually dispensed his Father's advice after healing a person. This advice varied with different individuals. I suggest that his practice be followed and we offer whatever practical advice the Holy Spirit prompts us to pass on. He might require us to mention some of the following matters.

1. The client could be encouraged to offer praise and thanksgiving. In Luke 17:11–19 Jesus added a spiritual

blessing to the physical healing of the one leper who returned with praise and thanksgiving. The client should continue to do this as a daily affirmation, for every day that he lives free from a former pain or disability is a day of special blessing.

2. When drugs have been prescribed, or the client has been receiving special medical care, he should visit his doctor for ratification of the healing and for specialist advice. This was Jesus' concern in Matthew 8:1–4.

3. It is good to point the client towards the next step in Christian commitment, whether repentance, baptism, receiving the Spirit, or joining a church. As the client will not normally be a believer (see page 49–51), it is usually right to explain the good news to him and introduce him personally to the Great Physician.

4. If the cause of the ailment was sin or if it was demonic, it may be right for this to be recognized and renounced by the client. If this is so, then pray with the client about the matter and help him to do this.

5. Further ministry will sometimes be necessary. I usually need to minister two or three times before results are tangible. I wish that I did not have to. I do not know why I have to. But I do. Explain this to the client and make plans for more ministry.

6. It is important to pray for the client's continuing healing, safety and protection. The enemy has been defeated, but must be expected to fight back.

7. Remember that Christ often commanded silence and so do not suggest the client testifies about the healing. If the healing is authentic it will be obvious to all, and if it is not authentic then he is better off remaining silent. The healing agent should also take care not to brag about what has taken place. Others' testimonies about how *they* have been used in mighty healings might draw oohs and aahs, but they rarely inspire faith. More usually they breed

## Graham Tomsett—Barcombe Parish Church, East Sussex

In May 1979 a lump appeared on twenty-nine-year-old Graham's neck. He had visited his doctor and was waiting for an exploratory operation when some blood test results announced the possibility of cancer.

Graham says: 'I then began the most rewarding time of my life. The operation showed that I had Hodgkin's disease and suddenly I was surrounded by a group of people praying for me and my young family. I only attended the local church occasionally for the sake of my children and could not be considered a believer. But as they prayed for me I felt my worries lift, and on admission into hospital I was amazed by the peace which overwhelmed me. I had abdominal surgery to remove my spleen, to examine my liver and my lymph nodes and the lower half of my body was anaesthetized for three days. After convalescence I began daily radiotherapy on my neck and chest.

'Shortly after starting this a friend suggested that I should pray myself. I was astounded, but as there was not much else to do I asked, 'Father, I believe you can heal me, and I ask you to do it now. Thank you. Amen.'

'Two days later the doctor called me into his office to say that, much to his surprise, the mass of cancerous cells in my chest had vanished.

'I was amazed, and cried all the way home. My amazement was not so much at being healed, but at being chosen to be healed. I knew next to nothing about God, but resolved there and then to rectify that deficiency.

'During the last seven years the disease has returned twice and I have had to undergo lengthy chemotherapy treatment. I look well, but the disease is still within me encased in a mass of dead cells, waiting to leak out. However, I have found God's purpose for life and know with certainty that his love overcomes all things.'

pride in the speaker and despondency, cynicism and disillusionment in the listeners.

## Healing during public worship

We have seen that it was quite exceptional for Jesus and the early church to heal during public worship, yet, strangely, it is commonplace today for leaders to move away from this biblical principle. Of course, it can never be wrong to pray for those members of the local body of Christ who are sick: these prayers could be for patience, strength, comfort, doctor's skill or recovery, but that is not the point at issue. In recent years large numbers of churches have introduced special healing services and regular times of ministry. God has used these to encourage healing, but I suspect that they are a necessary stage in the restoration of the healing ministry rather than its final format. It seems to me that the pattern and language of most contemporary healing services usually speaks more of blessing than of healing. There is nothing wrong with blessing. Indeed, I believe that the ministry of blessing should feature every time Christians meet together, but please let us use the correct word for what we do in our services. We inevitably create unnecessary disappointment when we advertise the ministry of blessing as the ministry of healing. (The *Ashburnham Insight* on blessing and cursing examines this in some detail.)

An advantage of healing services and ministry times is that they bring the ministry of healing right into the centre of a church's life, but such sessions should not be the focus of the ministry. One disadvantage is that, unless great care is taken, they suggest that the ministry rests in the hands of the leaders or the ordained. The gift of healing in 1 Corinthians 12:9 is primarily for use in public worship, but this gift does not reside in any one individual. As with all the 1 Corinthians 12 gifts, the gift of healing can be given by the Spirit to any individual believer in any service: he is a most capricious Spirit! 1 Corinthians 12:27–30 suggests that a few people will be given this gift so regularly that it develops into a ministry, but these folk will not necessarily be the ordained or the leaders; they might, and they might not.

I suggest that the laying on of hands for blessing or commissioning should be available at all services. Those with special needs can have hands laid on their heads to receive the blessing of peace, and those with particular pastoral or evangelistic tasks during the following week can have hands laid on them for commissioning so that they go out from, and in the name of the church. However, I believe that healing in services should only be administered following the normal scriptural principles for initiating a healing. Those who are prompted by the Spirit to request healing will naturally ask for ministry from a couple with proven gifts of healing, and all believers should be given the freedom to respond discreetly to a divine 'Go heal him' at an appropriate or predetermined point in the service. We must work towards the time when healing ceases to be associated with individualism and occasional services, and starts to pervade the entire life of the church, for seven days in every week.

## Healing in the world

### Believers in their beds

This is the only section of the church's healing ministry where leaders have exclusive authority. James 5:14 states, 'If one of you is ill, he should send for the elders of the church, and they must anoint him with oil in the name of the Lord and pray over him.' These verses have a limited application and are relevant only to two small groups of people: (i) the official leaders or elders of a local church; (ii) those believers who are too ill to attend services or visit the elders, and so need to have others contact the elders on their behalf.

James 5:14 does not authorize anointing by those who are not elders or leaders. It does not permit anointing by an individual priest or elder. It does not sanction the anointing of unbelievers, and it does not licence the anointing of believers who are not house-bound or bed-ridden.

This verse indicates that those believers who are so ill that they are unable to leave their house should send for the elders—plural, not singular. This underlines the principle of partnership in healing (see page 56). If there is only one ordained minister, he should not go alone but be accompanied by a leading layman, for example, a church-warden, steward or deacon. In large churches with many elders, I do not think all need visit, two or three suffice.

The elders should visit the severely ill believer in his home, taking with them a small bottle of olive oil. This can either be purchased at a local supermarket or collected from the diocesan bishop at the annual 'blessing of the oils' service held on Maundy Thursday. Both sources are equally effective, but the latter places the healing ministry more clearly within the life of the wider church. They may pour a small amount of oil on the client's head, or make the sign of the cross on his forehead using the oil, whilst speaking some relevant words, for example, 'We anoint you with this oil in the name of Jesus Christ, that you may receive the anointing of the Holy Spirit to heal your sickness.... (name the ailment). Amen.' Roman Catholic priests usually anoint both the head and the hands to stress that healing should result in service and most traditions agree that the oil should not be wiped off the person after the ceremony.

Anointing with oil is a symbol of the anointing with Holy Spirit and, as such, should only take place once. If further ministry is necessary it should feature only the healing touch and whatever words the Spirit suggests. The context of James 5:14 implies that confession of sin, forgiveness and faith-filled prayer should also take place at the time of anointing.

## Sinners in the streets

This is where the focus of the church's healing ministry should always be. In Mark 16:17–18 Jesus asserts: 'These are the signs that will be associated with believers: in my name...they will lay hands on the sick, who will recover.' Every believer who has been, and is, filled with Holy Spirit should be available to God as an agent of healing; should be ready to touch gently the ailing bodies of their friends, relations, workmates and neighbours, and announce to them the arrival of God's cure; should be regularly petitioning along the lines of Acts 4:29–30; and should be spending much time in silent listening, waiting for the divine initiative and instruction. When our unbelieving acquaintances are ill, our compassion should send us to our knees asking God to heal them and declaring our willingness to go and introduce his healing—if he desires to use us.

Christendom is divided between those who are overenthusiastic and those who are too reticent. God wants the enthusiastic to minister only when he prompts, and the reticent to ensure that they do minister when he does prompt. God wants our availability, our attention and occasionally our obedient action. When we receive a clear commission from God we should ask him to guide us to our partner, and clearly show both of us the how, where and when of ministry. I then usually telephone the client and say something like this: 'You know that I am a Christian. Ever since I heard that you were ill I have been praying for your recovery. You remember that in the Bible Jesus often directly healed people. Today he normally uses doctors and nurses, but he still sometimes heals independently of the medical profession, and I think that I have received an impression from God that this is what he wants to do for you. Would it be possible for a friend from church and me to come and see you tomorrow afternoon? We would like to pray with you and bring you God's healing.' They rarely refuse.

Sometimes God's prompting will be so urgent that we are called to bring healing in the street, on a bus or train, in a café or launderette. We have nothing to lose except our reputations: the person will not get worse; he might get better. And if we obey with sensitivity, gentleness, love and compassion, then the gift of our time and attention will in itself be therapeutic. The message that Christ cares will take root and begin to grow.

## The person who is not healed

Jesus healed everybody who came to him requesting healing, and he cured all those to whom the Father sent him, but the rest of the New Testament is not a record of unbroken success. There are at least four references which imply, or from which we can infer, either unsuccessful or unattempted ministry for healing.

In 2 Timothy 4:20 Paul sadly records, 'I left Trophimus ill at Miletus.' (Trophimus the Ephesian is mentioned twice in Acts as a trusted travelling companion of Paul.) In 1 Timothy 5:23 Paul did not instruct his favourite protégé Timothy to pray or have hands laid on him, but to 'give up drinking only water and have a little wine for the sake of your digestion and the frequent bouts of illness

## James Hammond—Hailsham, East Sussex

James has had a very painful rheumatic illness since early 1983. Through this and the steroid treatment he became very depressed. He was unable to use his hands and so lost his job as a graphic designer. He also gave up his position as a house-group leader, and his independence, and he thought he was losing his mind.

His doctor referred him to a psychologist and a local Anglican minister. The psychologist listened and enabled James to put things in perspective, and he found great comfort in these visits, especially as everything was in absolute confidence.

James' church helped practically by paying many bills, but also supplied many contradictory 'words from the Lord'. He desperately wanted to be better, but always felt that the responsibility for the lack of healing was being placed on his shoulders, thus adding to the pain of the illness. James says, 'I felt like an embarrassment. I no longer had to be healed for myself, but for everyone else's sake too. I was inundated with people practising every healing fad, and eventually I had to ask the elders to stop people from keeping on coming round to heal me. Every time somebody 'ministered healing'—and I wasn't—I felt awful. I thought that I had let them down. I know that most had real compassion, but so many seemed to need desperately to prove themselves. I felt less and less like a human being and more and more like a guinea-pig in some spiritual laboratory.'

James suffered greatly because of suggestions that being ill must mean he was out of the will of God; that he actually was healed and only needed to exercise faith and the symptoms would go; that he was not healed because he did not want to be healed, and so on. After a time of wanting to die James gradually came to terms with being ill. He can now say, 'I want to be better but it is no longer the most important thing. Knowing God is, and I am beginning to trust him much more.'

that you have'. Paul writes about his own eye ailment in Galatians 4:13–14, 'When that illness gave me the opportunity to preach the Good News to you, you never showed the least sign of being revolted or disgusted by my disease that was such a trial to you.' Finally, in Philippians 2:27 Paul records that the messenger Epaphroditus, 'has been ill, and almost died, but God took pity on him'. Does this mean Epaphroditus was miraculously healed, or is not a slow, natural recovery a more likely explanation?

It is instructive that these four sick men were all servants of God. Surely this endorses my earlier suggestion that God is more interested in the miraculous healing of unbelievers than of believers. Paul records no reason for this quartet's lack of healing and this must be some solace when we are faced with similar situations.

Disappointment is bound to face those who commit themselves to the church's ministry of healing, to those who pray for healing and make themselves available to respond to human requests and divine commissions. There will be those who are not healed, those whose initial healing lapses and those who are half-healed and then make no further progress. There are many questions and few answers. Sometimes, as I have suggested, the cure of our pride is higher on God's agenda than the healing of the client's disease; frequently we mishear God; and many times we act out of enthusiasm or in isolation. We do not pray enough, live simply or mix with unbelievers. We are ambitious, impatient and fascinated by phenomena. We stay safe in our narrow tradition or experiment with unbiblical matters like healing by proxy. We give up after a set-back, exaggerate with false claims, and worst of all we blame the client for the failure and pretend that his sin or lack of faith was the reason for the disappointment. Blame God if you must; blame yourself; but never, never blame the client.

In one sense it is not true that occasionally nothing happens. With God nothing is impossible, and if we recite his words and radiate his love then something must happen.

The gifts of our time and attention, our words and gestures, our prayers and caring all have healing value. This is not to escape the question of why no physical healing has taken place, but it is to avoid the pretence that nothing happened.

Sometimes, as with Abimelech, Miriam and the Shunammitess, the appreciation of the healing is delayed. And at other times the actual healing is gradual, as with Naaman, the Shunammitess' son, and the Mark 8 Bethsaida blind man. In cases like these there is no scriptural warrant for the teaching which suggests that clients should thank God for something of which they are unsure and unaware. That is hypocrisy, not faith. The arrival of the miracle depends more on the prayers of the agent than it does on the client's faith. This strange teaching about faith has arisen only because of the emphasis on healing believers. How can we demand faith from an unbeliever? Christ did not.

Matthew 13:58 informs us that Jesus could not work many miracles in Nazareth because of the general lack of faith, but the Scriptures also suggest that Jesus found the presence of faith in the centurion and the haemorrhaging woman to be quite remarkable. There is no record that Christ ever informed a person they could not be healed because *they* lacked faith. The fact that a person came to Christ requesting healing demonstrated their faith, and when we respond with obedience to a divine initiative, this evidences our faith. We do not need to imagine the person into being cured, or be thoroughly convinced that he will be healed (that is what the Bible means by hope, not faith). We are only called to speak God's words and perform his actions. On the few occasions that I have been absolutely certain an individual would be healed they have been completely unaffected. Yet at other times I have been riddled with doubt, and felt as dead as Elisha's bones, yet seen blind eyes instantly restored. The whole area is a mystery!

Many people turn to the healing ministry only when a loved one is dying, and then see death as a failure. Death is often the perfect healing and those who are involved in the church's healing ministry must have an adequate theology of death. Christ is as active in dying as he is in healing; and there can be miraculous deaths as well as wonderful cures!

From my considerable experience in this area (that is, when healing *doesn't* come) I make the following suggestions of things to say and do when after much ministry an expected cure still does not take place.

1. Have a prayerful de-briefing with your partner and go through the steps you took in the interview and healing action. Ascertain if you were obedient to every prompting; establish if you made mistakes or omissions.

2. Talk and pray the whole matter through with somebody more experienced in the healing ministry and ask for his suggestions.

3. If anything emerges from the de-briefing and advice-seeking, arrange to see the client one last time; otherwise ensure that a different pair ministers to them later on.

4. Praise God with the client for the lovely times of fellowship spent together.

5. Establish one thing that you have learnt from the episode and explain that to the client.

6. If the client is a Christian, get him to join you, or somebody else, in healing others. Remind him that in 1 Kings 19 Elijah was healed of his suicidal depression by being given three tasks of ministry to perform.

7. Find out what the client has learnt through the ministry and praise God together for that.

8. Ensure that neither you nor the client feels guilty about the lack of healing. Explain that sometimes God's priority is to prune the agent's reputation and pride; and laugh together about this.

9. Pray and fast for guidance.

10. Have a good argument with God as to why he made himself look so small and impotent.

11. Send the client a short note thanking him for his time, assuring him of your prayers for his healing, and suggesting something helpful for him to read.

## Forward into healing

Those with a fruitful healing ministry are the ones who have persisted through the barren years and months, who have gone on responding to the human 'please' and divine 'go', even when their experience shouted at them to stop wasting their time. After our reputations and pride have been crucified and buried, God sends his resurrection power. We stop trying, cease shouting, suspend the techniques that we stole off somebody else, and join the spectators who watch Christ heal the sick through us. Healing can be a heady broth to those who have not passed through the school of pain, but to those who have graduated with crucifixion honours, healing others is a deeply humbling experience.

Those with a fruitful healing ministry must also recognize that God heals in waves of power. For a few months everybody is healed; then for a few years nobody is healed; then suddenly it all happens again. This was Paul's experience in Acts 16–20, and it has been repeated throughout history in the lives of others whom God has greatly used. This pattern must be anticipated in our contemporary experience. The barren times should not be filled with agonized searching for hidden sins or some other cause, but instead they should be full of endless evangelism, holy simple living, and fervent prayer for God to work again in his power.

In every tradition and denomination, on every continent around the world, Christ has recently requickened a zeal for healing. So too has the devil. Demonic diagnosis and healing abound: Revelation 13 tells us that in the last days this will be so. In these days of fascination with all things strange, we need to be those who repudiate all healing (other than by the mainstream medical profession) which is not solely 'in the name of Jesus'. The question is not, 'Does it work?' but, 'How does it work?' and, 'Who is at work?' We need to learn the wiles and guises of the devil and to warn the world of the danger of involvement with such healing. But more important, we need to become those who can stand up with integrity and cry out loud that our God is 'Yahweh Rapha'—the Lord who heals.

Never has there been a more urgent need for the church's healing ministry itself to be healed, for the different traditions to learn from each other and to learn together from the Bible. Never has it been more important for Christians to pray for doctors and nurses, to support them, and to write letters of appreciative thanks when they have helped us or one we know. Never has it been so crucial for Christians to crucify their reputations, to trust the foolishness of God, and to be ready to touch the sick and speak commands of healing. Never has it been more critical for all Christian believers to cry out to God, 'Help your servants to proclaim your message with all boldness, by stretching out your hand to heal and to work miracles and marvels through the name of your holy servant Jesus.'

Our healing God needs an army of obedient, weak and ignorant servants who will only echo his healing voice and be his holy hands. My prayer is that you who have read this healing highway code will volunteer for the church's healing ministry. God only desires your availability: give him that and one day he may use you in a miracle.

*Personal Notes*

# Healing

## Healing in the Old Testament

*Abimelech*

*Miriam*

*Jeroboam*

*The Zarephathian*

*The Shunammitess*

*The Shunammitess' son*


*Naaman*


*Elisha's bones*


*Hezekiah*

## Jesus the Healer

*Who was healed?*

*What were they healed of?*

*Where were they healed?*

*How were the healings initiated?*

*How were they healed?*

*What happened after the healings?*

**The Healing Early Church**

*Who, what and where?*

*The initiation*

*The healing action*

*The consequences*

# The Context of Biblical Healing

## *Evangelism*

## *Simple lifestyle*

# The Church's Healing Ministry Today

*Preparation for the healing ministry*

*Ministering healing*

*Practical suggestions*

*Healing during public worship*

*Healing in the world*


*The person who is not healed*


*Forward into healing*